Living Art

Exercises for Igniting Creativity

Unleash
PRESS

Living Art

Published by Unleash Press

© 2023 by Unleash Creatives

Book cover design by Christopher J. Shanahan

Contributing Authors: Lisa Baron, Sascha Ealey, Ashley Holloway, Jen Knox

Edited by Ashley Holloway and Jen Knox

Featured Creatives: Perry Logan, Sandra Logan, M. H. Loyer, Vanja Kragulj, Jennefer Rousseau, and Dee Stribling

Printed in the United States of America

ISBN 978-1-7375194-1-6

Introduction

Create your life every day the same way you approach a piece of art—with creative abandon, curiosity, and enjoyment. Your life can be filled with creativity and artistic expression from the moment you wake and stretch to the time you drift off to sleep. Living creatively is about looking at the world with different eyes, and a new sense of wonder. This is what we wanted to offer you here. *Living Art* is a book filled with exercises, challenges, and myriad offerings that range from silly to serious. Feel free to read this book front to back, back to front, or just open it to a random page when so moved. Whatever your process, enjoy and try something new. Maybe you'll want to send us your own ideas about how to live artistically. We'd love to hear them.

So let's dive in ...

cre·a·tiv·i·ty
/ˌkrēāˈtivədē/

noun. the use of the imagination or original ideas, especially in the production of an artistic work.

−Source: Oxford Languages

Creativity as a Noun?

In this book, we see *Creative* as a noun*(you)* and invite the **verb**.

Let's **Create**.

Oh, but first, let's start with a few random facts about things that have nothing to do with creativity. Or, wait, maybe they do …

On timing ...

Waves transport energy, and energy takes time to build. Surfers know that timing is crucial, and they must wait for the perfect time to ride a wave.

As you read on, it may be helpful to remember that creativity comes in waves.

It's okay to pause a moment and wait for the next wave.

On starting when you're ready ...

Wood frogs adapt to freezing temperatures by allowing their bodies to freeze, too, thereby remaining in suspended animation. Don't consider **unfinished** creative projects abandoned, consider that they're in **suspended animation**.

On perfection ...

Kintsugi is the ancient Japanese art of repairing broken pottery using gold-infused lacquer to mend the broken bits back together. In doing so, this technique eschews the ever-elusive notion of perfection in favor of honoring the history of the object despite its perceived flaws. The marks of wear are seen as a sign of strength, valued as a record of events that took place during its lifespan, to be honored accordingly as pieces that make up the whole. What was once broken is not lost.

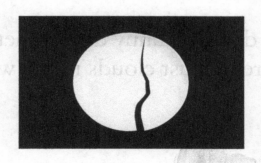

On Positivity ...

Creativity is something you can *feel*.
You know that feeling, when
something sparks your creativity, it's
almost as if something is *ignited* inside
you. *Pure. Bliss.* Right?!

But how do we achieve that spark?
What sparks the spark?

Research suggests that **positive**
emotions beget creative insight (which
also then begets positivity).

Every day is a sunny day; sometimes
there are just clouds in the way.

un·leash
/ʌnˈliːʃ/

verb. to suddenly let a strong force, emotion, etc. be felt or have an effect.

So how do we unleash creativity?

Unplug.

Creativity Needs Room to Breathe.

Breathe.

So much of our lives is spent in perpetual motion; we move from one thing to the next, to the next, to the next, taking for granted one of our most basic bodily functions: breathing. Yet we cannot achieve any of this *busyness* without our breath. Adults breathe, on average, 12-15 breaths a minute, yet how much time do you devote to actually thinking about your breath? *Zilch.*

So why not start now?

We won't call this *meditation*, because *meditation* carries expectations. Instead, we'll call this "being still."

Find a comfy place to sit. You don't need to sit cross-legged, just as long as you are comfortable. Set a timer for two minutes (yes, that's all!). Now sit. Breathe. Your eyes can be open or closed. Repeating a mantra can help, such as "I am breathing in, breathing in" on the inhale, and "I am breathing out, breathing out" on the exhale. Whatever floats your boat.

Taking time to consciously focus on our breathing helps to settle the mind and re-center ourselves. Often at those times when we feel like life is speeding up, it is better just to slow down…

Embrace your inner sloth.

P.S. Have you ever tried drawing your breath?

Try it!

Find a quiet space and bring some paper and pencils/markers with you. Find a comfy place to sit and spend a few minutes relaxing.

As you begin to notice your breathing, visualize your breath as a line. What color is it? Is it a straight line? Squiggly line? Thin? Thick?

Match the line with your breathing and begin drawing. Alter your breathing pattern to experiment with how this motion looks on paper. Use different colors, mediums, and types of paper. What does your breath look like?

Breath

Embrace Nature.

Take time to observe nature from wherever is convenient for you. This doesn't mean going to a park or the mountains. Find nature where you can—that stray dandelion that grows back no matter how many chemicals your neighbors spray on it, for instance. Observe a small piece of nature and how it shows resilience, unleashed, untethered, unrestrained, and completely unstoppable.

speaking of which,

remember **flow?**

Take a moment to think of a time when you felt in perfect flow. You delivered beyond expectations and enjoyed every minute of it…

Where were you? What were you thinking? What did you create and/or share on that day?

So what blocks us?

"My inner critic!"

"Your what? Never heard of such a thing."

(But if we had heard of such a thing, we'd try the following techniques.)

Create the IC.

Create a fictional character who epitomizes your inner critic. List all their attributes (appearance, likes, dislikes, fear, joys), then make them the villain in a short story. The list of questions on the next page might help get you started.

Freewrite for 20 minutes.

Interview the IC.

Try imagining your IC character and doing a little **interview** with them.

What does this person or thing or monster dream about?
Where does it live?
Fears?
Favorite color?
Favorite movie?
Favorite song?
Does it believe in ghosts?
Does it believe that singularity is inevitable?
Who does your inner critic look up to?
Favorite holiday?
Does it believe world peace is possible?
Does it have a day job?
What does it do on the weekends?
Why does it pick on you?

Now, imagine this was a job interview.
Would you hire this IC?

Fictionalize your IC's Twitter feed.

If your IC is going to be a PITA, so can you.

If your IC was a piece of IKEA furniture, what would it be?

Get Visual.

Draw or **paint** a picture of your inner critic. Here are a few examples from our authors...

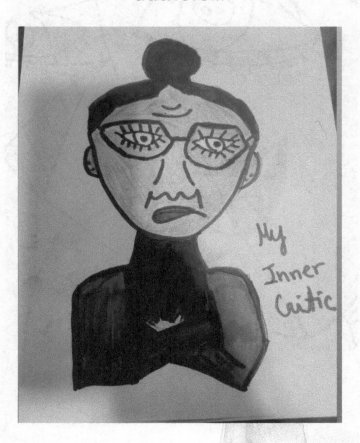

My Inner Critic

Reframe.

Below are three exercises to reframe your relationship with your infamous inner critic.

I.   Think of the **emotion** or **feeling** that you get when you feel **blocked**. Do you think things like "Argh!" Or "Oh no- Where's my muse?" Use the next twenty minutes to free-write or draw what comes to mind when you feel this emotion.

II. Write a letter thanking your inner critic for helping to protect you, but let it know you've outgrown it.

III. Imagine the batteries in your alarm clock ran dead, but as soon as you took out the old batteries to replace them, time stopped. What would your inner critic tell you to do? What would you do?

Bonus ideas!
When nothing else works, there's always cooking.

Inner Critic-eradicating Recipe
aka
S'mores

Ingredients: Graham Crackers, Marshmallows, Chocolate

Directions:
- Roast a marshmallow until gooey.
- Place on a graham cracker
- Place a piece of chocolate on top of that.
- Complete the sandwich with another graham cracker.
- Enjoy!

Q. How does this help with my inner critic?
A. Does it matter?

Oh, and **magic...**

Alchemy definition: a power or process that changes or transforms something in a mysterious or impressive way

2 spells for removing the inner critic from your workspace:

#1

Light a candle. Imagine your inner critic is the flame. Blow it out. Bam! No

#2

Make a list of all the things your inner critic says, and come up with a counterargument for each. Say each counterargument aloud, then burn the original list (safely, of course).

Exercise

The journey toward creative realization begins with self-awareness. The first step is looking squarely at what we have created in our lives thus far. By examining the patterns and habits that comprise our lives today, we can identify opportunities to refocus existing creative energy and carve out more time and mental space to make art, tell stories and innovate. Because creative energy dictates the way we live our lives, the exercises in this opening section are about simple observation and reflection. With a clear idea of where we are starting, we can begin to move forward by making small adjustments in the way we observe and interact with the world around us.

Day-to-day creative inventory

Exercise

Take the day ahead to reflect on all that inspires you and all that bores you in your day-to-day life.

Depending on your routine, you may want to try this on a weekday and again on a weekend. Jot down those times you feel bored or lacking in energy, and think about where you are and what you're doing.

Example:
8 a.m. - Commute: I'm either bored or angry.
2 p.m. - Hangry: I need a snack to stay awake at the day job. If I have to answer one more email...

Next time you recognize one of these times (in the moment), take the opportunity to do something different. If you normally check email at 2 p.m., take a short walk, or start up a conversation with a co-worker instead. If you are normally stuck in the car, see if you can find new music to listen to and work on your singing voice.

Journal about what you did differently.

Living Art

Living Art

What about fostering creativity?

Well ...

(We mean this with all due respect. Try taking a shower!)

DID YOU KNOW THAT 72% OF PEOPLE HAVE CREATIVE INSIGHTS IN THE SHOWER?

—Wired to Create: Unraveling the Mysteries of the Creative Mind by Carolyn Gregoire and Scott Barry Kaufman

Creative cooking.

Think about creativity and cooking. Garlic?
Ginger? Turmeric? Have you tried Garam Masala?
Let your creativity go wild in the kitchen.

Create a recipe for creative confidence– anything goes.

Example:

Ingredients: 2 cups of love
1 tablespoon of vision
A pinch of encouragement
1 gallon of grit

Mix it all up, then eat chocolate.

Let go!

Writing or drawing with your non-dominant is a way to tap into deeper parts of the creative self?

Pivot from your "usual."

Opposite day

Studies show that implementing a new routine can help foster creativity. So why not have an *opposite day?*

Have dinner for breakfast and breakfast for dinner. Start your day with dessert. If you normally drive to work, take transit or walk. Re-read your favorite book as an audiobook. Change your dog-walking route. You get the picture…

Visualize

Visualize a prism. When an idea floats into your mind, consider all aspects of it as if you were studying all sides of a prism.

On the next page, draw a prism.

Prism exercise:

Make squiggles!

Gather a pencil and some blank sheets of paper (No erasers allowed). Without thinking about it, use the pencil to draw a squiggle anywhere on the page. Now, turn that squiggle into a drawing of something: is it a dolphin? A school bus? A man on horseback?

Let your imagination take hold and see what you create.

Your squiggle.

Did you know?

The song *Under Pressure* by Queen and David Bowie was mostly improvised and the result of an impromptu visit between friends. While illicit substances were likely involved (which we do not condone), this demonstrates how great things can stem from serendipity.

-Far Out Magazine

Clean Sheets

Clean sheets are awesome. Crisp white cotton stretched tightly over feathery softness? It feels great. It feels new. Best. Sleep. Ever. *Right?!*

Clean sheet redesign is actually a thing in the business world. It is a method of rethinking problems that stand in the way of efficiency or productivity through imagining what things may look like free of the current restraints. Kind of like putting clean sheets on the bed.

This same thinking can be applied to creativity blocks. Instead of obsessing over how to get *through* the block, what if you looked at creative blocks as clean sheets of paper? Reinvent that creative block and make it *work for you* instead.

Clean sheet of paper.

On (im)Perfection ...

We accept imperfect vegetables (and sometimes seek them out for being budget-friendly), so what's wrong with imperfect art?

Who decides what constitutes being 'perfect' anyways?

As humans, we strive for normalcy.

(Take it from these cats, no human is normal.)

Write about beauty of oddities.

On Impostor Syndrome.

hint: real impostors don't have syndromes about being imposters. they're too busy being impostors.

Make a list of things in your life you didn't believe you could achieve, but you did. Finishing school, finding and being in a healthy relationship... expanding your creative life. Despite some challenging twists and turns along the way. YOU made all of those things happen.

Below that, list all the qualities you bring to your own creative life that continue to make you valuable.

List I: I didn't think I could do …

List II: Qualities that moved me forward.

Did You Know?

Engaging in creative artistic expression has been linked to better health.

-Source: Stuckey & Nobel (2010)

Befriend Your Creative Self.

What do you tell a creative friend who questions their talent?

Tell yourself the same.

Revision is Creative!

The song *Hotel California* by The Eagles (1977) was originally titled "*Mexican Reggae*"?

This just goes to show you that it's OK for creativity to evolve.

Gifts.

List the gifts creativity has offered you.

"The gift of exploring my journey through life with a sense of wonder and enthusiasm."

–Dee Stribling, Former Poet Laureate of Hillsborough, North Carolina

You at the day job.

You when writing your novel.

You, waiting in traffic.

You, after you painted your masterpiece.

Color

outside of the lines

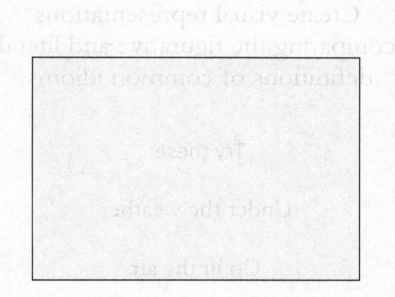

Visual
prompt

Create visual representations comparing the figurative and literal definitions of common idioms.

Try these:

Under the weather

Up in the air

Bite the bullet

Ride shotgun

Creative Living.

Register for an activity or class you wouldn't normally take - something outside your comfort zone. Maybe it's a burlesque class? Or painting portraits? Pottery? Macrame? Tai chi?

Your hidden talents just might surprise you.

Remember the days you finger-painted
with chocolate pudding?

**Let yourself get messy. That's
where creativity lives.**

exercise:

SPLATTER PAINTING!

Word Association.

Take a word association game to the next level: Start with a regular word association, such as:

carrot>stick

Then carry it forward to create new connections:

stick>dog>leash>walk>shoes>
running>sweat>bed…

(*winkwinknudgenudge*)

Tip

Find someone who jiggles your Jell-O, and spend time with them.

(Get your mind out of the gutter… Think platonic, not plutonic).

Creativity is best when shared.

What distinguishes humans from robots and artificial intelligence?

Creativity. Creativity is what makes us human.

Journal about artificial intelligence and its potential role in creativity.

Practice.

Creativity takes practice.

The more you practice being creative, the more creative you will become.

Now go practice.

Prompt:

Instead of making a 'bucket list', try your hand at making an anti-bucket list of all the things you would *never* do.

Things I'll never do...

1.

2.

3.

4.

5.

6.

7.

8.

9.

10.

Unleash Creative Courage.

Check in with your inner child ...

#1. Describe a typical day in the life of your inner child.

#2. What activity from your childhood do you miss that you could incorporate into your adult life now?

#3. Draw a picture of your inner child with your non-dominant hand.

#4. Ask "Why?": Kids are constantly asking "Why?" because they are curious and are constantly learning. You can begin by questioning what you want to create. *Why must you make it? Why with that particular medium? Why now? Why here?*

#5. Mimic! Kids often learn by copying others. If you're learning a new craft, there's nothing wrong with studying how artists before you succeeded by trying out their style or voice (*sans* plagiarism, of course). Embrace your inner Mynah bird!

Remember being a kid playing with toys or with friends outside on the playground?

Remember when everything felt like an adventure? You were the Grand Storyteller! The Creator of Worlds! You were both villain and hero! Calling all pirates, sorceresses, astronauts, aliens, cowpokes, and sheriffs!

Throw caution to the wind and go play like a kid again.

Use your kitchen utensil, pots, pans, and containers as instruments and experiment with the different sounds. Create some funky music and host a kitchen dance party.

"At 10 I was freer, not limited by others – Possibilities were endless! I drew pictures on everything – I was going to be an artist! I lived in a place where children ran free, ate wild berries throughout the day, and came home when the street lights came on. We were untamed. We built forts, braided grass, learned to swim in the river, ran in packs, climbed trees, flew kites, and laid in the long grass watching the clouds go by. But life wears you down, people tell you what you can or cannot do, barriers are placed in front of you…life can be challenging, creativity can get bogged down under the pressures of life. But lately, as I surface up from middle age I'm feeling creativity return, not quite as free, and definitely in a much more complex world, but it's there. I'm trying new things, not limiting myself, finding time to daydream again. And, I'm realizing I have more patience, more wisdom, more desire to stick with the complexities of creativity. In fact, I see more possibilities and am regretting my lost middle years where creative pursuits seemed frivolous."

-Sandra Logan
Knitter, crocheter, baker, houseplant nurturer, painter, problem-solver

Safe Spaces

Think of a place you found safe and cozy as a child. Where was that? What did it look like/feel like to be there?

Take steps to recreate that space or draw it and place the drawing next to your computer or in your art studio.

When we feel safe, we feel free to let go.

My creative safe space looks like …

Unblock
Vulnerability.

image by Sascha Ealey

What are your thoughts about the relationship between vulnerability and creativity? Journal and/or draw about these thoughts.

Purpose.

Without purpose, art flounders. Let's focus on determining and/or revisiting our deepest creative drive. At this stage, we look beyond what we want to create to uncover the true reason we feel called to create. This is a highly personal or spiritual practice for some of us. For others, it is about the value of entertainment and positive emotions.

Listing our motivations and identifying our intended audience, be those readers or end users, will enable us to connect our projects to our projected impact. Simon Sinek's *Start With Why* is often referenced for its foundational concepts for sustainable business; try to identify your creative "why" and explore the value of returning to it when you lack inspiration.

Make a list of resources.

Include all the people, places, and things that motivate you to create.

Motivation list.

1.

2.

3.

4.

5.

6.

7.

8.

9.

10.

Vision...

begins with a belief that things can change. In this chapter, we will dream big and without apology. We'll put our creative brains to work by imagining and reimagining what we'd like to create for our lives. Imagining an ideal future in which our creative ideas are at work in the world is not only fun, it also allows us to expand our possibilities. This means going beyond a simple sentiment, such as "I'd like to write a novel someday," and instead visualizing what life would have to look like to show up creatively each day and write, to go on a book tour, and to sit down with readers to discuss what you've created. With a new mindset around our creative work, we'll put the vision to work by setting one small target that will get us just a little bit closer to the dream. With self-awareness, purpose, and vision, we notice that we are living with more creative intentions each day.

Celebrate.

How do you celebrate creative wins?
How did you celebrate as a child?
a few ideas...

Dance

Sing

Keep creating

Tell the world

Do a cartwheel (careful, folks)

Your Turn.

Notice how we've been sharing quotes?
Well, it's your turn.

Come up with your own quote about
creativity. Write your personal creative
purpose in the space on the next page.

Your **Quote**:

"

"

(If you need inspiration, check out the following pages.)

"Geometry is one of the foundations of mathematics. The patterns of the world and how to recognize them are creative."

–Chris Shanahan
Artist, economist, and publisher

Story

You can write your "now" story.
You are not your old story.
You can spin a piece of who you were and who you hope to be…
choose the colors, fabric, thread, and spin away.
There is no seamless life.

–Lisa Baron
Writer and educator
Originally published in *The Blotter* (Chapel Hill, NC 2019)

This pinot grigio-incited revelation led me to ask myself "Why *must* I progress from scarves to toques, to socks, to mittens, and then, by golly, even *sweaters*? Why can I not simply stick to making scarves?" Scarves offer a sense of accomplishment and satisfaction. I start with a ball of yarn, and just… knit. I can make the scarf as wide or as long as I want. If I run out of one color, I can change it up with another easily. I can create any pattern I wish. When knitting a hat or a sweater, you are limited by size; the pattern dictates when the project is finished, but with a scarf, I get to decide. It doesn't need to be perfect either; no one would notice if it weren't. Besides, there is a certain honesty in imperfection. There is just such… freedom in knitting a scarf. Social narratives of the middle-aged be damned!

-Ashley Holloway
Writer, crafter, educator, mother, spouse
excerpt from *Knitting my Boredom Away*.
Originally appeared in *The Globe & Mail*

"A famous writer once showed me his rough draft for a story that was published in a very notable publication. He said it was draft 1 of 17, and it was, quite frankly, a mess. This vulnerability squashed the myth that some people are just creatively gifted and reminded me that creativity is a process. Thank you, professor."

–Jen Knox,
Author and educator

"I never thought about how I defined creativity before, but I would compare it to problem solving. When I'm writing, I think, *how will I get people to want to read this*? When I'm cooking or baking, I think, *how will I get people to crave this*? When I'm creating art, I want people to want to look at something and like it. My creativity is also a little competitive. It's alive. It wants to win. It observes reactions. It can change and pivot. I'm often told I'm creative when I thought I was actually problem-solving…even if that problem is just making a dinner that two kids will eat or hosting a party that includes vegans."

-Jennefer Rousseau
Universal Design for Learning consultant

"Being creative helps me escape. Or maybe, it brings me home to myself… in any case, when feeling or expressing my creativity, my mind and body are freed. It has a meditative quality. The magic of creativity for me is in how it recharges and soothes me. I think creativity brings people together. To be creative is to move forward, to solve puzzles, to answer questions, to wonder…When people gather around creative pursuits it is for good, for joy, for making this world a bit better.

My granddaughter learned to finger knit when she was five and as she sat beside me, both of us absorbed in our knitted creations, she sighed and told me that her very favorite place to be was right there, in that moment, side-by-side with me and our yarn."

-Sandra Logan,
Knitter, crocheter, baker, houseplant nurturer, painter, problem-solver

"At the start of my journey as a children's book illustrator, I sought to find an outlet for my creativity through my work. As illustrators, we tend to seek validation from the outside world for our work, whether it's from our peers, social media, or our clients. This often stifles our creativity because we end up producing work that we think others will like or that others will pay for. This can result in a lot of suffering.

I soon realized that I had to find other outlets for my creativity and to let work just be work. The amazing thing is that when I allow myself time to be creative outside of work, it trickles into my work; I end up more inspired and as a result I create some of my best work. Being able to let go allows me to embrace my most creative, weird self to come up with work that is true to who I am. I think this is where the magic is. I think this comes from confidence in what you do."

-Vanja Kragulj
Illustrator

"I still find it hard at times to believe that I've crossed over to being a creator of a medium (writing) that people will enjoy and actually purchase. At times I'm humbled, and at other times I feel empowered to be able to entertain my readers. Having found the passion to write a little later in life, (55) I still do not see myself at par with many of my peers simply because I still have such a sharp learning curve. There are times when I do feel a creative satisfaction and other times when I feel that I still have so much to learn. When people ask me how I finished writing two books, I simply tell them to keep writing and to do what you enjoy. The rest will take care of itself."

-Perry Logan
Author, *Kids of Concern Trilogy*

"Having earned a paycheck in three different countries throughout my adult life —none of which were the country of my childhood or education — I see creativity as the secret sauce that flavours my work for employers who appreciate my unique perspective. Being from "not here" gives me the freedom and confidence to create both my own identity and my own approach to solutions and market them successfully."

-M. H. Loyer
Educator, poet, mother, mentor

History and society would have us believe that creativity is a gift bestowed upon only a lucky few, or that it should follow a particular pattern or narrative. Likewise, some may believe creativity can only take on visual forms. This book proves that once unleashed creativity can take remarkable shapes and forms in art and day-to-day living.

Remind yourself of your creative prowess often, drop comparison and competition, and remember that no one else can create what *you* can. Creativity belongs to everyone. That means you. Own it!

A Call for **Your** Creative Ideas from, *the* Unleash Team

We are constructing a page of creative living for our readers. Consider submitting your insights about creativity to **info@unleashcreatives.com**

Jen Knox

Jen was a high school dropout who went on to find purpose through writing, which led her to earn a BA in English from Otterbein University and MFA from Bennington College. Her short fiction and essays are taught in classrooms and appear in over a hundred publications around the world, including *The Best Small Fictions* (edited by Amy Hempel), *Chicago Tribune, Chicago Quarterly Review, Room Magazine, and The Saturday Evening Post*. Her collections include *The Glass City* (Prize Americana winner), *Resolutions* (AUX Media), and *After the Gazebo* (a Pen/Faulkner nominee). Jen's chapbook of flash fiction, *Dandelion Ghosts*, was released in 2021, and she is currently working on a craft book about how to write compelling fiction. Jen's first novel, *We Arrive Uninvited*, is one of the top-rated projects of all time on Coverfly's Red List for family stories. It won the Steel Toe Books Award in Prose and will be released in Spring 2023. After teaching creative writing for over a decade, Jen began to coach writers 1:1 and offer idea-to-publication services through Unleash Creatives, which is now a holistic arts organization.

Ashley Holloway

Residing in Mohkinstsis, Ashley Holloway teaches healthcare leadership in Calgary, AB. She is a nurse with a Master of Public Health, a graduate diploma in Global Leadership, with further studies in intercultural communication and international development. Ashley's work has appeared in the Calgary Public Library *Short Story Dispenser*, *The Nashwaak Review*, *The Globe and Mail*, *Magna Publications*, *The Prairie Journal*, *CARE Magazine*, *Flash Fiction Magazine*, *Canadian Dimensions*, with regular contributions to *Lead Read Today*; forthcoming publications include *Flash Fiction Magazine*, and *WELL READ Magazine*. Ashley has co-authored two books with her writing partner extraordinaire, Jen Knox (*Create & Curate: 500 Ideas for Artists & Writers*, 2023; and *How (Not) to Lead*, 2023) and reads manuscripts, writes book reviews, and provides editorial feedback for Unleash Press. Her work has been nominated for the Pushcart Prize.

Lisa Baron, PhD, LCSW

Lisa Baron is a teacher, writer, social worker, and mentor. She earned her Bachelor's in Teaching, (University of Wisconsin-Madison) her Master's in Social Work, (University of CT), and her Doctorate in Philosophy from the Institute of Clinical Social Work (Chicago). Lisa also teaches creative writing for Story Circle Network. Some of her work can be found in Tales-From-The-Pandemic, The Blotter, Social Work Today, and Real Women Write: Beyond Covid Leaning Into Tomorrow (Story Circle Network). Currently, Lisa splits her time between the Chapel Hill, North Carolina area and Chicagoland. She is most proud of her long-term marriage to Lee, and her three wonderful adult children and their partners. Find more on her website.

Sascha Ealey

Sascha Ealey was born and raised in Brooklyn, New York, where she still resides with her two children. She wanted to become a writer ever since the age of seven. She obtained a bachelor's degree in English at Saint Francis College in Brooklyn Heights. One of her dreams was to use her life experiences to help young women feel understood in a world where society wants them to sweep things under the rug. Sascha wants to challenge and encourage women to step into their truths despite the opinions of others. It is her hope that young girls and women break those generational curses that were left by their ancestors. She released two books in 2022, *Dry Bones* and *Broken Glass*.

Also available from Unleash Press …